# THE BEST OF
# ESSENTIAL ELEMENTS
### FOR JAZZ ENSEMBLE

## 15 ARRANGEMENTS FOR YOUNG JAZZ ENSEMBLE

ISBN-13: 978-1-4234-5221-8

Visit Hal Leonard Online at
**www.halleonard.com**

# ALL OF ME

Flute

Words and Music by
**SEYMOUR SIMONS** and **GERALD MARKS**
Arranged by *MICHAEL SWEENEY*

# FLUTE

## Rhythm Workout

Bah   Doo Dot          Doo Bah Dot   Doo        Doo Dot

Bah   Doo Dot       Dot  Doo Bah Dit   Doo     Doo Bah Doo Bah

## Melody Workout

## Chord/Scale Workout

## Demonstration Solo

# MISTER COOL

Flute

By Mike Steinel

# FLUTE

# JA-DA

Flute

**Words and Music by BOB CARLETON**
Arranged by MICHAEL SWEENEY

## FLUTE

# SONG FOR SAN MIGUEL

Flute

By MIKE STEINEL

FLUTE

**Rhythm Workout**

doo doo doo bah    doo doo    doo    doo bah    doo    doo         doo doo doo bah    doo doo

doo    doo bah    doo doo bah                    doo doo doo bah    doo        doo

doo doo doo bah    doo    doo    doo doo doo bah    doo    doo    doo    doo    bah

**Melody Workout**

**Scale Workout #1**

CONCERT G NATURAL MINOR SCALE

**Scale Workout #2**

CONCERT G HARMONIC MINOR SCALE

**Demonstration Solo**

# SUNDAY AFTERNOON

Flute

By Mike Steinel

# FLUTE

## Rhythm Workout

## Melody Workout

## Scale Workout

## Demonstration Solo

# TAKE THE "A" TRAIN

Flute

**Words and Music by**
**BILLY STRAYHORN**

*Arranged by MICHAEL SWEENEY*

SOLO FOR ANY INSTRUMENT

D.S. AL CODA (WITH REPEAT)

CODA

# FLUTE

**Rhythm Workout**

**Melody Workout**

**Chord/Scale Workout**

**Demonstration Solo**

# BUBBERT'S GROOVE

By MIKE STEINEL

Flute

# FLUTE

## Rhythm Workout

Doo Dot    Doo Dit                    Doo    Doo Bah    Dot    Doo Bah                Doo Dot

Doo   Dit                    Doo  Doo  Doo  Doo    Doo  Bah

## Melody Workout

## Chord/Scale Workout

## Demonstration Solo

# PERFIDIA

Flute

**Words and Music by
ALBERTO DOMINGUEZ**
*Arranged by MICHAEL SWEENEY*

# FLUTE

## Rhythm Workout

## Melody Workout

## Chord/Scale Workout (Concert B-flat)

## Demonstration Solo

# BALLAD FOR A BLUE HORN

### (Feature for Trumpet or Alto Sax)

Flute

By MIKE STEINEL

# FLUTE

## Rhythm Workout – (articulate lightly)

## Melody Workout

---

**Helpful Hint: Interpreting solo passages in jazz**

Often we are asked to play a "solo" in a jazz piece that is not improvised but rather interpreted in a personal style ("stylized"). In these situations try to maintain the basic melody notes and focus on varying the rhythm of the written part. The demonstration solo is a good example of this technique.

---

## Demonstration Solo – ("Stylized" treatment of melody m. 5-20)

# SATIN DOLL

Flute

By DUKE ELLINGTON
Arranged by MICHAEL SWEENEY

## FLUTE

# SO WHAT

Flute

By MILES DAVIS
Arranged by MICHAEL SWEENEY

# FLUTE

## Rhythm Workout

Bah Doo Bah Doo Bah Doo Bah Doo     Bah Doo Bah Doo Bah Doo Bah Doo Bah

## Melody Workout (A Guide for Improvising)

## Scale Workout #1 – Concert D Dorian Scale

## Scale Workout #2 – Concert E♭ Dorian Scale

## Demonstration Solo

# BUBBERT GOES RETRO

Flute

By MIKE STEINEL

**Rhythm Workout**

**Melody Workout**

**Scale Workout #1**

CONCERT C MAJOR BLUES SCALE

**Scale Workout #2**

CONCERT C BLUES SCALE

**Demonstration Solo**

# BASIN STREET BLUES

Flute

Words and Music by
**SPENCER WILLIAMS**
*Arranged by* MICHAEL SWEENEY

# FLUTE

## Rhythm Workout

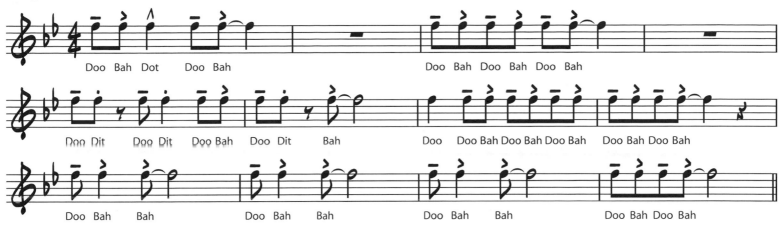

Doo Bah Dot  Doo Bah          Doo Bah Doo Bah Doo Bah

Doo Dit  Doo Dit  Doo Bah  Doo Dit  Bah          Doo  Doo Bah Doo Bah Doo Bah  Doo Bah Doo Bah

Doo Bah  Bah          Doo Bah  Bah          Doo Bah  Bah          Doo Bah Doo Bah

## Melody Workout

## Scale Workout

## Demonstration Solo

# ON BROADWAY

**Words and Music by BARRY MANN,
CYNTHIA WEIL, MIKE STOLLER and JERRY LEIBER**
*Arranged by MICHAEL SWEENEY*

Flute

# FLUTE

## Rhythm Workout

Doo Doo Doo Doo Bah  Doo  Doo Bah  Dit  Doo  Bah

Doo Doo Doo Doo Bah  Doo  Doo Bah  Doo Doo  Doo

## Melody Workout

## Scale Workout

MIXOLYDIAN SCALE

"MAJOR" BLUES SCALE

## Demonstration Solo

# BLUES FOR A NEW DAY

By MIKE STEINEL

Flute

# FLUTE

## Rhythm Workout

Bah Doo Bah Doo Doo Bah   Doo Dot                                    Bah Doo Bah Doo Bah

Doo Bah Doo Bah   Doo Bah              Bah Doo Dot   Bah Doo Bah Doo Bah   Doo Bah Doo Bah   Doo Dot

## Melody Workout

## Scale Workout

MAJOR BLUES SCALE                    BLUES SCALE

## Demonstration Solo